Naked
by Egypt

authorHOUSE®

AuthorHouse™
1663 Liberty Drive
Bloomington, IN 47403
www.authorhouse.com
Phone: 1 (800) 839-8640

Published by AuthorHouse 02/22/2018

ISBN: 978-1-5462-2856-1 (sc)
ISBN: 978-1-5462-2873-8 (e)

Library of Congress Control Number: 2018901752

Print information available on the last page.

For Charisse

Contents

I Have Something To Say

I have something to say
Can you hear me?
You can't stand in my way
What do you see?
24-inch weave,
Long nails painted red,
Don't worry about who I lay next to in bed,
Listen to what I said.
Judge me by what I stand for
Not what I wore
Bantu Knots are not my style
Does my outer appearance
Determine my acceptance
I am a POET
A child of God
Anointed vessel
Don't miss out on the message
By the devil's distractions
Receive the package
Don't judge a poet by the cover
I am an ARTIST
My words speak volumes
I make your mind wander
Hear me,
See me,

Look past your disbelief
I won't be boxed
I don't have to wear faux locks
To get my message across
This is how I'm supposed to look
This is how I'm supposed to write a book
I'm not held to your limitations
I meet Gods expectations
I am a POET
I can't be moved
Stand behind my words
Inspire the youth
I'm here with you
I have something to say
You can't imitate
Or intimidate.
Stop staring at me with your shady eye
Stop with your negativity
You're afraid I'll rise
Someday I won't be a theory
You will have no choice but to respect me
My success doesn't mean your defeat
Join the legacy
Stood on my feet
From the strength of praying on my knees.
I'm not like you.
That's why you persecute
My voice is undeniable
Faith unquestionable
This message is for you
I'm here to shake up the universe

Make you uncomfortable
I wasn't supposed to be here
Against all the odds
This is more than a career
Purpose
Who can I fear?
Don't make up your mind off what you see
It's more than what you get
Don't miss the prize worrying about what it's wrapped in.

Nothing To Do With Me

It has nothing to do with me
You're fighting against your own insecurities
If I win
It doesn't make your light dim
I make you uncomfortable
I'm a reminder of what you haven't accomplished
But it's not too late
Lingering time with self-hate
Jealousy in disguise
I was always present in your demise
But suddenly, I'm the problem?
I've switched up?
But you switched up
Before I had change
There's enough room for the both of us.
I did it for all of us,
We had trust
Making it was just a plus
Talent wasn't made for only one person
There are enough people to touch
Someone is willing to listen
You just have to open up
We were going to run the world
No Beyoncé you were my girl
Sister.

Two of a kind.
I knew your secrets you knew mine
Brown like me
Strong like me
Talks to deep
Cries to sleep
Pain I keep
Betrayal I peeped
Mama said it was jealousy
In disbelief
What did I have
That I wouldn't let you have
It wasn't mine it was ours
Cause you were my girl
And you remained that
As I elevated into a woman
Separation
Because I was chosen
My dream had my dedication
Thought I was leaving you out
I'm meeting new people what is that about?
"Why you can't take me?"
The rants and shouts
Constantly weighing me down
All your negative energy
Behind your fake ass smile
All your gossip
Behind your fake ass, '"Ima be down".
Only coming around for ammunition to gun my character down
You said I'm not walking with the people I crawled

But I was walking when you met me 5'5 ft tall,
Saw your true colors
None of them light at all
Sad that the light at the end of the tunnel won't see you at all
I got hipped to your schemes
Stop with your subliminal messages and memes
You played the fool
Your planned backfired on you
Trying to tear down what's special about me
You lost what was special about you.

Black & Blue

Blue is pretty too,
And so is the color purple
You are complete
Even blue moons are fully circled
You are whole
Authentic ass gold
Unequaled.
The grass on the other side
Broken backs and silent cries
Few people visit
Respected by the twisted
Darker the berry the sweeter the fruit
They ran off with your juice
Call it their own now its cleared for use
You capture our history
You flash the truth.

57th Street

He found me on 57th street
Tall brown and handsome
Personality that captures minds
A smile that triggered mine
You moved me.
You couldn't of came at a better time
My spirit was dehydrated
And you refreshed me,
Held me,
Caressed me,
Made love to my brain
I orgasmed mentally
Unintentionally
You had that effect on me
Kept me moist without even touching me
The truth on 57th street
Everything I asked for
Street credentials
With deep dimples
You had character
The nigga even had respect for his mother
Under that glitter he was hurting
Soon I saw what I was in for
God always unveils the curtains
Kept secrets and spoken lies
He didn't even apologize
Forgiving him for shit he wasn't even sorry for

I still gave fellatio until my jaws were sore,
Thinking as he ejaculated
That he would fill up with love for me
He only cared about him and 57th street
His hand was the easiest to hold
And the hardest to let go
I had to learn from him to grow
He had some fucked-up qualities
Willing to die for the flag
Kept a side bitch with a fat ass
I came 2nd to 57th street
I wasn't coming 2nd to no bitch
The grass isn't greener on the other side
It is greener where you water it
I wanted him to make me his home
To make him moan
I wanted him to want me
I wanted him to need me
I needed him to trust me
I trusted him to keep me.
He failed I don't even think he tried
We connected one time
And our souls were tied
He ignored it
Or didn't feel it
I started to regret him
Passive aggression
I doubted him
"What you doing?"
"Who you with?"
Felt like I was on some stalker shit

Miserable
Unreliable
Hurt people,
HURT people.
Ironed his clothes
He left my heart wrinkled
Heard of his reputation on 57th street
Aware but he was gentle with me
Kept that other side in the streets
Eventually, 57th snatch him away from me
He had a bond with 57th street
He could never belong to anybody
She always cried out for him
Slaughtered his homies
Kept him from his son
She taught him to hold on to his gun
He can't hide, he can't run.
He was signed up to 57th street
Obligated to her
Sworn to her pain
Refused to let him go
Not even 57ft in his grave
I wanted something different
She wants it to stay the same
Tug of war
Our soldier.
She had the victory
Her property
I was out of bounds in her territory
I broke free
And now I'm staying clear of any nigga on 57th street.

Layers

Let me shed a couple layers of me
So, I can have room for layers of you.
Let me show you the impossible
The different layers of my roles
I can be anything
I can be everything
Keep your eyes on me
Do you trust me?
Come join me
I'm where you're supposed to be
Expose your heart
Unwind your mind
Let your doubt depart
I'm your guide
Let me in
Shed a couple layers of you
So, you can have room for layers of me
Slice your pride
I'll cut mine
Release your pain
Break out of the chains
Walk through the darkness
Pierce the light
Don't be frightened
We're going to be alright
Let me shed a couple layers of me
So, I can have room for layers of you,

Step into who you're meant to be
Grasp your purpose
See what I see
Wipe your failures
They don't define your character
Drop your guard
We have come too far
I'm going to shed a couple layers of you
And you're going to shed a couple layers of me
With the bond of God
As husband and wife, we will be complete.

What Are You Listening To?

What are you listening to?
Lies or the truth,
Do you do as they say?
Cover your eyes and look the other way
Our youth are dying
Cities are crashing
What are you listening to?
Do you see the gun smoke?
The agony
Babies crying for working mothers
And murdered daddies
Growling bellies
Sucked in from starvation
Reality sets in
No conversation
What are you listening to?
Media bullshit
Reality shows exploiting pastors on the pulpit
Black people, we're dying
Mass murder genocide
Families are broken
Our women objectified
"Shake that ass hoe,
Let me see how fast it can go".
Off this lean and coco

Can't get it up
Stroke my ego
"I'll throw you some mo dough",
Giving demands
Make me feel like a man
While I have kids, and won't even provide for them
Hip-hop where's the positivity
Awareness for HIV
What are you listening to?
I know you can hear the struggle to
Open your eyes
Expand your thinking
It's more than partying and drinking
Bentleys and Benjamin Franklins
America.
Home of the free,
Built off slavery,
Land of dreams,
And clean water isn't a necessity
What are you listening to?
Not the revolution
You don't know the problem
How can there be a solution?
Vampires of equality
Demonstrators of democracy
We don't matter
That's what you're telling me
What are you listening to?
Where are the options for black men?
Any acceptance other than gangs and violence?
Abandoned programs for the less fortunate

Year-long wait list
Zero options for the homeless
The run around from the government
A buck over poverty
Help decided by your salary
Who are they listening to?
Do you hear the people?
Equal opportunity isn't made simple
No money for the handicapped
Or the mental
They paid taxes and worked for this country
Stingy with the SSI money
It's easier to communicate
But harder to integrate
Trayvon Martin, I see my son in you
For a parent to bury their child is unnatural
That's not how life is supposed to go
Deadly trip for a beverage and skittles
No arrest and he was told to stand down
Nobody is at fault but you're on the ground
What are you listening to?
Sabrina Fuller's protest for justice
Or how Zimmerman wasn't convicted
Oscar Grant, I see my brother in you
Gone to soon what did you possibly do
Life snatched by the law
Judicial system flawed
Claims of reaching for a taser
One bad call took you from your daughter,
Who's going to be her father
Who are you listening to?

Who's getting through to you
Can you see the problem?
I'm bringing as much awareness as I can
We will get justice for Sandra Bland
Black on Black crime is always an issue
But when the cops kill us there not labeled as criminals
Officer Dan receives paid leave
While our peoples blood dries the streets
Sandra Bland, Oscar Grant, Mike Brown
Trayvon Martin and every life lost
I'm speaking on your behalf at any cost
This poem is for you
They will be who you start listening to.

Flourished

This is the very first time
Massaging my walls,
Exploration of me inside,
I'm not hard to please
It's clear what my body needs
The urge.
My flower flourished
Muscles throbbing
Beating heart
Blossoming like it's springtime in March
Explore through my body
Mood setting
Ron Isley,
Palms sweating
Thighs gapped
Vibration as I relax
Specific positions
Movement manipulations
I found the motion
The perfect sequence
Paralyzed.
Mouth opened wide
Climaxed reached
Exhale and release.

Everything But Daddy

Do you know how it feels?
When you're breaking down,
And you're in a constant battle because someone depends on you,
I couldn't afford a heartbreak
I couldn't mourn mistakes
Too much on my plate
It was like I was on another planet
Unbreakable space
Only 19
The world was on my shoulders
An infant on my hip
Becoming a mother wasn't seen as an achievement
Abortion recommended
Sarcastic questions
No explanations
Was I a statistic?
Please, God, don't let my mother be disappointed
What will my friends say?
How will they look at me?
Outcast,
Exile.
Expected to graduate first and have the baby last
The pain you put me through,
She was pregnant too.
Doctor said there are no more options for you
Mary J. Blige got me through

Done crying over the shit you do
My child is not an accessory
You say he's not the last of your priorities
You have proven he's the least of your worries
He does not need you
He needs a parent.
Being a single mother wasn't a part of the plan
I'm growing up with this angel and your absent in the struggle
You didn't raise my son
So, when he shines like one
Don't bother to come
It's going to be the same old absent father song
You're not my father I only have a mom.

Hold me

———— ✦ ————

Can you hold me?
I want you to inhale and release me
Just to do it all over again,
I want us to have one scent
US the fragrance
I want to watch foreign TV
Because were the only thing we need to understand
Find skin on my body you have never touched before
Make it familiar
I want my back arched to your stomach
And my rear to your pelvis
Let your arm go numb
Because I won't let go
And I want you to be ok with that
Because at that exact moment I need you
I want to eat cheap dinners
Because I'm full off you,
I want to kiss you with the butterflies of a first kiss
And the anticipation of the last kiss before our wedding
I want a honeymoon every day
I want puppy love every night
I want to sit up and do nothing
But talk about something
And be open to anything
I want to be happy
Can we just be happy?

It was a Tuesday

It was a Tuesday
A normal LA day
Coffee and French toast
Brunch on the west coast
Feeling fancy
Deposit my check
Money withdrawal
Got the late shift
Had some extra time
Checked out Starbucks Wi-Fi
Connected.
Seen you connected.
We connected.
I see you
Noted
It was Tuesday
You smiled at me
Eye contact and exchanged energy
Chiseled jaw
6ft tall
Body language said hi
Vibe said come here
But we stood there
You took your coffee to go and left me
Stuck in a daydream
Thinking about today
About that guy, I almost met on Tuesday.

The Love Of A Single Mother

How am I supposed to teach you how to be a man?
I'm still learning how to be a woman.
I ask myself how was I chosen
How was I chosen to complete a task that's bigger than myself?
How can I take care of a lil boy that's going to be bigger than myself?
How did I meet the qualifications to be your mother?
I fell in love with you when you were as light as a feather
Strong as a rock
When I laid eyes on you my heart stopped
Then it started beating again and I learned how to love the correct way.
Unselfishly, unconditionally, you are gravity to me
19 years old just trying to keep it together
Singled out because your father didn't want to be a father
Your whole existence is a reflection
The love you give me lets me know I'm going in the right direction
The air you breathe gives me reassurance
I can see our future in your eyes
I think about all the things I want to give to you
And it saddens me that I couldn't give you an active father
I'm the one who had to show you how to fix your collar
You taught yourself how to ride a bike

You taught yourself how to fight
Self-taught at 7 years old
Your father couldn't even teach his self how to transform
into father mode.
7 years old and your already more of a man than your dad is
You don't lie about loving me, you have more heart than
your dad did
I put my soul into molding you into a decent human being
You're so smart,
I want to make sure you know all your letters and work on
your reading,
I want to fix that attitude you get for no reason,
I want to help you become a morning person,
I want to fix every negative habit you inherited from me.
I will be understanding because I know your obstacles
Everything you are, is me, down to your follicle
I will know your struggles because they are my struggles
I'm going to instill the values my mom instilled in me
Put God first,
Earn your degree,
Find a profession you'll love to be
Understanding life can never be planned and that everyone
doesn't deserve a second chance
Stay away from those fast ass girls
Make mistakes and make sure you learn
Do what you must do now, so you can do what you want
to do later
Of course, be better than your father
And finally,
Know it always gets better and nothing last forever
Except the love of a single mother.

The Supreme

You see what I see in myself
Uncontrollably in control
On the rise
Makes men want to pay me their tithes
Desiring to give me a baptism in their waters
To filthy up their sheets right after
I can make eyes follow when their heads don't
I can keep your attention
In a supreme dimension
Follow my whispers
I'm the supreme
Woke.
An American dream
1st pick on the team
Go as high as the championship
The dream team
The Supreme me
It's effortless to your surprise
Processing my fluorescence
Blooming into conscience
The Fever
I'm the sanctuary for the non-believers
My presence demands your awareness
My voice commands your advantages
Supreme being,
I'm the supreme.
Crown parallel to my breast

His favorite position is my head on his chest
Confident women respect it
Imitating what they can they just can't grasp it
The magic.
I'm the first and last stitch of the fabric
They can't understand it
Looting my essence and you still can't birth it.

Gamer

I didn't like Eminem for a long time because you did.
I didn't like video games anymore because you did,
I wanted to do the exact opposite of you
So, I could have a 0 percent chance of being anything like you
I didn't understand who fractured my life until I was an adult
You should have had a record before you were old enough to vote
And I was ruined before I even learned to float,
Age 8 is time stamped in my memory for eternity
Forever and a day.
I think I'll still remember when heaven open it gates
I hope you're not there
You can't be
I know God says forgive
But he can't be talking to me
This must be an exception
I wish somebody would have caught him
My mommy always told me I could tell her anything
But how could I tell her I don't even know what happened to me
What do you call you touching me?
Putting your teenage hands on my innocent body
Destroying me with your curiosity
What was this act that made me feel like a visitor in my own body?

My processing wasn't experienced enough to do anything
You thought I was sleeping
I was fully woke
The pain was fully woke
My fear was fully woke
It's still here as an adult
Does your wife know that she married a child molester?
A childhood destroyer
Does she know that those hands that she holds at night?
Are the very ones that almost ruin my life?
Do your friends know to never leave you around their daughters?
Does your wife know that she shouldn't make you a father?
You didn't get your day in court
They said it would of broke big mama's heart
Everybody's feelings were taking into consideration
Everybody's but mines
Out of sight out of mind
While nobody wants to talk about it
I can't stop thinking about it
Staying in a child's place I stayed quiet as a church mouse
There are too many rugs in this house
My innocence rest under one of them
Buried.
I attended my own funeral and resurrection in the same day
I laid down as a child and woke up with my innocence in another place
To add insult to injury nobody asked if I was alright
Not talking about your pain doesn't make it go away
Not pressing charges because they're family doesn't make tragedy ok

These are the ingredients
That ruin lives and keep family secrets
Now that I'm a parent I'm extra cautious
You were my boogie man I won't allow one to come out my
sons closest
Karma said you would have a fucked-up life
The one you deserve
I don't want an apology or a word
I want you rot under that rug where my innocence was left
It should be familiar,
It's where your secrets were swept.

They Say Never Meet Your Heroes

They say never meet your heroes
But she was my song sparrow
With a voice box of elegance
And a mind of diligence
I wanted to be her.
She had those eyes you could see yourself in,
Her past in,
Her present in,
The kind you could see her future in
She was a star.
The sun
The one
With every song, I could feel what she was feeling
We were connected, it was like I could feel her heart beating
With passion and grace, I felt every run and high note no
matter how far I was sitting
But being six years old I was always able to get a seat front
and center
Only family can enter
I was proud to be your goddaughter
Playing with your gold bangles wishing you would give
me one
And one day you did, one of the smaller ones
That bangle was my prize I vowed to never take it off
Being 6, of course, it got lost

I thought to myself I wonder how much this cost
Because in my eyes you were rich, nothing less than a boss
Have you ever been let down by the person that inspired you to be great?
The one that fed you cereal and offered everything on her plate,
The one that gave you hugs that made you feel like everything was ok,
The one that didn't care if you stayed up until 3 am to play
Do you know what you meant to me?
You were who I aspired to be
How were you influenced so easily?
I hadn't seen you in a while
But when I was 15 I got to see that smile
It wasn't the same
That light that made you the spotlight
Had exploded into flames
I couldn't wrap my head around the reason you kept shaking
God mommy why were you shaking?
Why aren't you singing?
Our hugs weren't the same
You smelled unfamiliar,
You looked peculiar,
I was looking into the eyes that told me I could be anything
The same eyes that had now disappointed me
The same eyes you must face every day
I think you get high because your reflection changed

I pray for you
I ask for understanding
because the only God can bring you back
But maybe I can give you, what you gave me
Inspiration.
Can I have my hero back.

I Will Be Wrong

Every man that has had a significant role in my life has left me,

Has hurt me,

Has disappointed me,

Has disrespected me,

I really tried for you.

I put my heart into it

It still wasn't good enough

I can't believe I got broken up with

Maybe my assignment was just to help

Or did you step on me

Being bitter slows the healing process

This is the last poem I'm giving you

It's insulting to tell someone what best for you is to be without them,

Reconstructive heart surgery

I'm holding my own hand from now own

I shouldn't have to suck my belly in around you

I cleaned everything in my house when you left

I didn't want to smell the aroma you left

I believed everything you said

Holding on to every syllable you spoke.

Trying every trick to not sleep alone

I don't care who's right just come home

Is this still your home?

I'm right, but for you, I will be wrong.

Gridlock

Let's say all the things we never say
Go day by day watching the clouds fade
Anointed in each other's scent
Gridlocked in commitment
I see no one else.
Every word I spoke was true
Every movement I choreographed on your body was my truth
Expressing my courage trusting in love again,
Mental notes,
Mechanical strokes,
Corny jokes,
Saliva soaked,
But for some reason you couldn't love me properly
Is God sending a divine sign that we should give up or is satan giving us a run for our money
Deep thoughts about my immaturity and potential
Questioning if the reward is worth the fight
Am I worth the battle to continue the war
Listening to Mary saying she not gon cry,
While I cry.
This is not what eyes were made for
Letting all these females know your single
You never told them you were taken
Doing the bare minimum to stay forgiven
Sometimes less is more but in this case less is less
Residue of tears shadow my face as I'm wishing you the best

Your walking out on me for the same shit I've forgiven you for
I can't take the silence.
Your anger lets me know I still have your attention
So, have you thrown in the towel
Are you going to throw back the love you found?
Is it only a matter of time before you turn your back?
Leaving me with your cold shoulder and alternative facts
I just wanted to exchange my world for our world
Be your girl
Hold on to your word
Are you going to miss us getting faded while the sunset faded?
Now you take your blunt in the living room
You're simply not in the mood
I desired to cook you home meals while you enter saying honey I'm home
Instead I'm left alone noticing my honey is gone
Where's that love you promised me
A sitcom love,
A sickening love,
A healing love,
A secret love,
A no secret love,
A courageous love,
That I don't have to say it because your think thinking the same thing love,
A race to the remote because we want to watch different things love,
Finding new things on your body I'm in love with love,
A respect love,

An I'll change that if you need me to love,
An acceptance love,
An I found me when I found you, love,
A wish you would have stayed love,
A how could you stop loving me, love,
A what am I going to do without your love?
Love.

Why Did You Wake Me?

We have talked about you disturbing my sleep
What's so urgent?
It's no secret
Our love has plummet
That's still no excuse to wake me
I don't see it as romantic at all
Rubbing the crust out of my eyeballs
Getting snapped back to reality
On where we stood before I went to sleep
I was on a mini vacation from you
I was free from infidelity,
Your current felonies,
The crying babies,
And your excuses to be lazy.
I was on pause
Body caged in these walls
We go through storms like the Caribbean
You used to wrap me like expensive linen
Your first trophy
Before you had me, I was worthy
I'm fed up but starving for attention
Ears next to my mouth and you still won't listen
Sleeping is my drug of choice
A series of dreams that gave me a voice
I have to be free somewhere

I sleep all day because I don't want to be here
The doctor said I'm depressed
I thought I just needed some rest
I don't respect the sin of taking your own life
I escape day and night
Until I get the courage to leave you in this lifetime
You didn't even notice my highlights
To busy watching the NFL highlights
We used to run the streets in the night light
Now all you do is disappear in the moonlight
Never returning before midnight
What happened to our date nights
And quality time
Who is on your mind
You used to look at me like I was your sunshine
I just want some appreciation
Your heart to be dedicated
It feels like a delusion
Is going our separate ways the only solution?
You didn't come up with a better conclusion
I wasn't in your equation
Even though our situation was unique
You cared more about getting paid than me
My fear is seeing you with someone else
But I'm tired of making it work baby
I'm tired of making you hurt baby
I want you around for us
And not just for the kids
I'm waiting for you to realize it gets no better than this.

Dear Alijah

Where can I start
How do I end
Alijah, you are the start
And the end
The sun sets with you in mind
And rises to see you one more time
The air is here for you to breathe
Relaxation is here for your peace
The word is here for you to teach
The people are here for you to reach.
I am here to be your mother,
You're here to keep me stronger
This whole world is manipulated to your advantage
A strategy in God's plan for your greatness
There a generation you must save
A couple ways you must pave
History, you must make
Special dates, I must save
I am already proud
Unconditional love I found
I didn't need anything else
I had you all for myself
I know I'll have to share with the world eventually
They need your cure for creativity
Strength from my side of the family
I never felt like you were half of me
Cause I sacrificed all of me

So, you can transform into a better me
I'm going to hold memories
And watch time
Although your only five
The clock is rotating by
The time is going to come
When Alijah Jaiden Clark must wake them up.

Printed in the United States
By Bookmasters